Extraordinary Victory for Ordinary Christians

If you want to discover and experience all that Jesus died to give you, this book shows you how. *Take it seriously!* What Ron Dunn teaches is biblical, practical and—believe me—remarkable. If you want God to make your life a miracle, learning and living the truths in this book is the way to start. I highly recommend it.

Warren W. Wiersbe
Author, a former pastor of Moody Church
and teacher on *Back to the Bible* radio program

Ron Dunn was a dear friend. He helped me understand the life of victory. I have read this book a dozen times in its original printing. The cover is broken, the pages are bent and highlighted. These truths have encouraged my heart for years. I am so grateful for CLC reprinting a book I believe is a classic in the Keswick line of teaching. You will be blessed beyond measure if you learn to apply the truths contained on these pages.

Michael Catt
Senior Pastor, Sherwood Baptist Church—Albany, Georgia
Executive Producer, Sherwood Pictures

Ron Dunn has provided an incredible volume which contains his journey from the struggles of infant faith to the fullness of triumphant faith. Though facing challenges most of us only read about in others, he stayed firm in his faith and in his confidence in the Word of God. His life reflected his lifelong determination to obey God regardless! Read these pages and you will find yourself making that journey with him . . . and you will never be the same!

Jimmy Draper
President Emeritus, LifeWay Christian Resources

Ron Dunn challenges us that "all Christian living is simply a matter of response." He highlights what our life journey with God can be like if we get to know Him—the giver, sustainer and reviver of life. Whether you're a new believer or have been a Christian for a long time, this book will encourage and energize you in your walk with the Lord. For, as Ron says, "Staying free [is] as much a part of [your] salvation as being set free." I highly recommend this book to anyone who wants to experience a revived, renewed and refreshed walk with Jesus!

Byron Paulus
President, Life Action Ministries

EXTRAORDINARY

Victory

for

ORDINARY CHRISTIANS

Lessons in Living from the Book of Joshua

RON DUNN

Published by CLC Publications

U.S.A.
P.O. Box 1449, Fort Washington, PA 19034

GREAT BRITAIN
51 The Dean, Alresford, Hants SO24 9BJ

AUSTRALIA
P.O. Box 469, Kippa-Ring QLD 4021

NEW ZEALAND
118 King Street, Palmerston North 4410

Extraordinary Victory for Ordinary Christians
ISBN 10 (trade paper): 1-936143-16-X
ISBN 13 (trade paper): 978-1-936143-16-0
ISBN 10 (e-book): 1-936143-46-1
ISBN 13 (e-book): 978-1-936143-46-7

TO . . .

The Members and Staff of the MacArthur Boulevard Baptist Church of Irving, Texas, with whom it was my great joy to serve nine years as Pastor.

—For saying one memorable night in April: "If you're crossing over, we want to go with you."

—For saying one triumphantly tragic holiday: "We're here and we care."

AND TO . . .

Joanne Gardner, my Secretary for those nine years and my Friend for life.

CONTENTS

Foreword

I first heard Ron Dunn at a Bible Conference in Kansas City, Missouri, in 1975. He had recently buried his oldest son Ronnie, who had taken his life on Thanksgiving Day. While Ron was obviously devastated, there was a victory in his voice like I had never heard, as he preached from Romans 8:28. It was one of the most powerful sermons I've ever heard. As a young seminary student, I knew I wanted the power that was obviously present in his life.

I became a "fan" of Ron Dunn. I don't apologize for that. He became, from a distance, a hero to me. When he was in the area, I would go to hear him in conferences and revivals. I have pages of notes from his sermons. I have every tape of every message available. There hasn't been a day since his death that I haven't missed him.

In 1976 the book you hold in your hand first came into print. I quickly wore out my copy. It is falling apart, the pages are marked up, and I have used more than one illustration or principle in sermons throughout the years. These truths about the victorious life are desperately needed today. Ron didn't just write and preach about it, he lived it. He was a walking illustration of the power of the truths he taught.

I am grateful for the vision of CLC to reprint this classic. It's been out of print far too long. I'm grateful for their vision to get other books by Ron back in print. Though he is dead he still speaks, and what he has to say is powerful. I had the privilege of hosting Ron for sixteen consecutive Bible Conferences. Much of what he taught our church is still bearing fruit in the 21st century. We maintain his website www.rondunn.com because we want a new generation to hear and read this giant among God's men.

If you long for victory and desire to cross over into the fullness of life as God intended it, read this book. The principles contained on these pages are clear, concise and biblically based. The truths within are basic to experiencing that extraordinary victory you long for. With this book Ron did not give us a typical commentary on Joshua. He's given us a book with meat on the bones, life flowing through the ink and power on every page. He shows us the courage of one man, Joshua, and how he learned to believe God.

Michael Catt
Senior Pastor, Sherwood Baptist Church – Albany, Georgia
Executive Producer, Sherwood Pictures

Introduction

Anything Would Be Better Than This!

I once heard Stuart Briscoe compare the life of the average Christian to an old iron bedstead—"firm on both ends but sagging in the middle!" The statement intrigued me, not because it was catchy but because it described perfectly my own Christian life. I knew I had been saved—firm on that end. I knew that when I died I would go to heaven—firm on that end. But, boy, was the middle sagging! I was on my way to heaven, but I wasn't having a heavenly time getting there.

I was the "successful" pastor of a large and growing church in a booming suburban area. We would have had to lock the doors to keep from growing. But my success was like that of a reducing aid salesman whose customers lose weight while he gets fatter and fatter. My preaching was helping everyone but the preacher.

I was in good company. Many of the preachers I knew were in the same boat. But that provided little comfort, and I often cried to the Lord, "There has to be more to it than this. I don't know what I need, Lord, but I need something. Anything would be better than this."

As always happens when we become desperate enough, the Lord answered that prayer. This book is the outgrowth of what He taught me in response to my prayer. I am indebted to the people at Master's Press [the original publisher] for their patient assistance; to my sister-in-law, Mrs. Julie Blevins, for an invaluable suggestion; and to my wife, Kaye, who always encourages me and who spent many long hours correcting and typing the manuscript.

God desires that every Christian experience the life of victory. While the Bible admits defeat, it never assumes it. The predominant theme throughout Scripture is victory, and anyone living less than victoriously is falling short of the divine intention.

One of the clearest pictures of the life of victory is found in God's dealings with Israel. Paul tells us in Romans 15:4, "For whatever was written in earlier times was written for our instruction, that through perseverance and the encouragement of the Scriptures we might have hope." And again in First Corinthians 10:11, describing their wilderness experiences, he says, "Now these things happened to them as an example, and they were written for our instruction, upon whom the ends of the ages have come."

The book of Joshua is God's object lesson or victorious living. It tells how Joshua, taking charge after the death of Moses, led the people out of the wilderness of defeat into the Canaan of victory. And the amazing thing is that we move out of our defeat into victory the same way Israel did. In this book is revealed God's *modus operandi* for a full and exciting Christian life.

Come with me on a journey with Joshua into a land of abundance. We will cross a river spilling over its banks in flood, watch massive city walls fall at our shout of victory, see dread giants overcome—all pointing toward the victorious life awaiting every Christian. It is not Joshua's journey only—it is yours and mine.

One

THE REAL THING

A preacher I know was speaking at a Bible conference on the theme of victorious living and was invited to be interviewed on one of the local radio stations. After introducing him to the radio audience, the M.C. said, "Now, Doctor, you call what you preach the 'victorious life'; is that correct?"

"No," said the preacher, "that's not what I call it."

"Oh, I see. Well then, you call it the 'deeper life'; is that correct?"

"No, sir, that's not what I call it."

The announcer started to speak, hesitated, then asked, "Doctor, what do you call what you preach?"

"I call it the Christian life," the preacher answered.

My friend was right. A victorious life is not a superior brand of Christianity reserved for the elite of the elect. It is the normal life for every Christian. It isn't bestowed upon some because they are spiritual; it is given to all because they are saved! Too many Christians are struggling to win a victory that has already been won. It was won two thousand years ago. The Christian life is a victorious life and anything less is a cheap imitation of the real thing. Jesus said, "I came that they might have life, and might have it abundantly" (John 10:10).

It will help if we understand that the Christian life can be divided into two stages—the Red Sea stage and the Jordan River stage, with a wilderness in between. What the cross is to us, the Red Sea was to Israel. It was the symbol of their redemption, their deliverance from the bondage of Egypt by the mighty hand of God. They looked back to the Red Sea as we look back to the cross; they celebrated the Passover as we celebrate the Lord's Supper.

But it wasn't enough to get them out of Egypt. Moses reminded the people in Deuteronomy 6:23, "and He brought us out from there [Egypt] in order to bring us in, to give us the land which He had sworn to our fathers." The purpose of their redemption wasn't realized until they entered the land of Canaan. And to enter that land they must cross the Jordan River—then, and only then, would the redemptive purpose of God be fulfilled.

This may surprise you, but Canaan never symbolizes heaven in the Bible. Church hymns may say that, but the Bible doesn't. There were giants in Canaan—there are no giants in heaven. There were battles to be fought in Canaan—there will be no battles in heaven. God's people sinned in Canaan—in heaven all traces of sin will be erased.

Canaan represents the fullness of salvation, the fullness of blessing, the possessing of our possessions. Canaan was what God redeemed Israel for, just as victory is what God saved us for. He brought us *out* that He might bring us *in*. Many Christians are *out* but not *in*. They, like those spoken of in First Corinthians 10:5, die in the wilderness without ever experiencing the life of fullness in Christ.

*The victorious life is not one emphasis in the Christian life; it **is** the Christian life.*

The Old Testament describes Canaan as a land flowing with milk and honey, a land of luscious clusters of grapes and pomegranates and figs. The New Testament describes our Canaan as:

> Peace which passes all understanding (Phil. 4:7);
> Joy unspeakable and full of glory (1 Pet. 1:8);
> Blessed with every spiritual blessing in Christ (Eph. 1:3);
> More than conquerors through Him who loved us (Rom. 8:37).

Are you *in*?

The first nine verses of Joshua tell us three important things about the life of victory.

> Every place on which the sole of your foot treads, I have given it to you. . . . Be strong and courageous, for you

shall give this people possession of the land which I swore to their fathers to give them. Only be strong and very courageous; be careful to do according to all the law . . . be careful to do according to all that is written in it; for then you will make your way prosperous, and then you will have success. Have I not commanded you? Be strong and courageous! Do not tremble or be dismayed, for the LORD your God is with you wherever you go. (Josh. 1:3–9)

Victory Is the Goal of the Christian Life

Recently I heard someone refer to the victorious life as "an emphasis." It is not one emphasis in the Christian life; it *is* the Christian life. That is why in this book the two terms "Christian life" and "victorious life" will be used interchangeably.

As we have already seen, escape from servitude in Egypt was not God's goal for His people. He took them *out of* Egypt in order to bring them *into* their own land, the land He had promised them. Generations before, God had made this promise to Abraham as Abraham stood looking over the strip of land between the Mediterranean Sea and the Jordan River: "Lift up your eyes and look from the place where you are, northward and southward and eastward and westward; for all the land which you see, I will give it to you and to you descendants forever" (Gen. 13:14–15). Freedom from Egypt was only the first step. Until they occupied Canaan they would not experience God's complete rescue operation.

In the same way, God's goal in saving us is not to get us out of hell and into heaven—that's just a bonus. The real goal is for us to experience all that He has promised us in Christ. This is not an incidental emphasis in Scripture, but its heart. Listen to Paul speaking to the Roman Christians: "For whom He foreknew, He also predestined to become conformed to the image of His Son" (Rom. 8:29). To the Ephesians Paul revealed the goal of salvation in these words: "He chose us in Him before the foundation of the world, that we should be holy and blameless before Him" (Eph. 1:4). Not a word about hell or heaven there.

Paul wrote to the Christians at Colossae about "the mystery which has been hidden from the past ages and generations; but has now been manifested to His saints . . . which is Christ in you, the hope of glory" (Col. 1:26–27). In all God's dealings with you, He has been leading you up to His goal—the full release of Christ in you. That is your only hope for a glorious life.

Paul makes another point about victorious living in his second letter to the Corinthian church: "But thanks be to God, who always leads us in His triumph in Christ" (2 Cor. 2:14). It is possible for a Christian to always be victorious. Since the Lord Jesus can give you victory for a minute, He can give you victory for an hour; if for an hour, then for a day. If He can give you victory for a day, He can day by day give you victory for a lifetime. Anything less than always triumphing in Christ is less than God's desire for you.

But wait a minute. Does living in victory mean we no longer sin? Not at all; but it does mean that we learn to depend upon Christ for every aspect of our life. We live in His strength, not our own. We serve His desires, not our own. We live for His glory, not our own. And when we sin, instead of plunging into despair and guilt, we trust His cleansing blood to wash it away and restore us to that sweet fellowship. We become supersensitive to sin, and when the Holy Spirit convicts us, we immediately deal with it.

Many Christians read the promises in the Bible with enthusiasm but never really expect to see them fulfilled in their own lifes.

The best way to define the victorious life is to describe it, so let's examine some of its ingredients.

First, *we enter into God's promises.* The promises of the Bible become experiential instead of merely theological. God's promises to Joshua were definite. He told the Israelites the land was theirs; they needed only to act—act with strength, courage and obedience. And the promises made generations earlier were fulfilled before their eyes.

I'm afraid many Christians look at the promises of God as I looked at the Sears Catalog as a boy. When I was about ten, I spotted a .22 rifle in the catalog, and I had to have it! It cost twenty-five dollars, but it might as well have been a thousand. Knowing it was beyond my reach, I would get out the catalog, turn to the page that displayed the picture of "my rifle" and dream. No wonder the catalog is called "the wish book"—I wished and wished, but I knew I couldn't have it.

And to many Christians the Bible is just that—a wish book. They read the promises with enthusiasm and shout "Amen" when they are preached from the pulpit, but never really expect to see them fulfilled in their own lives. But the Bible is not a wish book; it is a faith book. And for those who, by faith, cross over into victory, all the promises of God become real.

Another characteristic of victory is that *we experience God's presence.* One of the promises God made to Israel which is repeated often in this chapter is "I will be with you." They would experience His continuing presence. God would be real to them.

In seminary I read a sermon by R.W. Dale, the famous preacher of Birmingham, England, in which he said, "Christ is as real to me as the chair on this platform." I thought, "Wouldn't it be great to be able to say that and mean it!" I knew Jesus wasn't that real to me, but I longed for Him to be. Praise the Lord, when He answered my desperate cry for help, one of the first things I experienced was the overwhelming awareness of His presence. Jesus became more real to me than any chair on any platform!

The third ingredient is that *we exercise God's power.* God promised Joshua, "No man will be able to stand before you all the days of your life" (Josh. 1:5). He was telling Joshua that no man could prevent Israel from reaching their God-appointed goal. Joshua would have the power to do everything God asked him to do.

When the original spies went into the land, they cowered like grasshoppers before the giants of Canaan. But Caleb, standing on God's promises, declared the giants would be bread for them. "Pass the peanut butter! We'll make sandwiches with them." And a generation later, as Israel acted in God's power, they found Him spreading a banquet table for them. God's power gives us victory over the giants in and around us. We become not only giant-defeaters but also giant-eaters! There are three aspects to this power.

Resurrection Power: "I pray that . . . you may know . . . what is the surpassing greatness of His power toward us who believe . . . in accordance with the working of the strength of His might which He brought about in Christ, when He raised Him from the dead" (Eph. 1:18–20). Think of it! The same power that raised Jesus from the dead is made available to every believer. You're facing a problem. Which is easier—solving that problem or raising a dead man from the grave? The answer is obvious. If God can raise one from the grave, He can do anything. You have resurrection power residing in you.

Reigning Power: "Those who receive the abundance of grace and of the gift of righteousness will reign in life through the One, Jesus Christ" (Rom. 5:17). God has made kings out of slaves and princes out of paupers. And notice, the verse says "in life," not in heaven. He's not talking about the "Sweet Bye and Bye" but the "Nasty Here and Now"!

Released Power: "And for this purpose also I labor, striving according to His power, which mightily works within me" (Col. 1:29). The life of victory means that I no longer labor according to my strength but according to His. My ability is no longer measured by my power but by His. Throw the word "impossible" out of your vocabulary. You can do anything and everything God wants you to do. There is nothing that can prevent you from being exactly what God wants you to be. No wonder it's called the gospel—good news!

Victory Is a Gift to the Christian

Victory is not only God's goal for the Christian; it is also His gift to the Christian. "Every place on which the sole of your foot treads, I have given it to you, just as I spoke to Moses" (Josh. 1:3). Notice the tense: "I have given," not "I will give." It was already theirs. God had given the land with all its riches to His people before they even saw what it was like.

Understanding that the victorious life is a gift already given us by God is essential. This means victory is *assured.* There is no reason every Christian cannot live a life of victory, because it is not attained by struggling and striving. It is part of your birthright as a child of God. You don't have to make peace with failure or come to terms with defeat. The victory of Christ is yours for the taking.

God's people are often slow to believe this—slower even than non-Christians. In chapter 2 of Joshua, Rahab, an insignificant citizen of the soon-to-be conquered city of Jericho, said to the spies:

> I know that the LORD has given you the land. . . . For we have heard how the LORD dried up the water of the Red Sea. . . . And when we heard it, our hearts melted and no courage remained in any man any longer because of you; for the LORD your God, He is God in heaven above and on earth beneath. (Josh. 2:9–11)

The enemy knew they had lost before the Israelites knew they had won! They had more faith in the power of God than God's people.

Since victory is a gift from God, it is already *accomplished*. Before Joshua led the people into Canaan, God said to him, "I have given it to you." Though the land was occupied by the enemy, it was God's, and He had given it to His people. Every step Joshua took was on conquered ground. And that's what the life of victory is—walking on conquered ground. Christian, every step you take today will be on ground conquered and controlled by our Lord Jesus Christ.

Victory Must Be Gained by the Christian

After my going to great lengths to say the victorious life is a gift, you may think I am contradicting myself when I say it must be gained. But the Scripture holds to both concepts. God told Joshua He had already given them the land but they would have to possess it and that would require strength and courage. Although the gift was absolute, it had to be appropriated. There was something for them to do.

This same idea is enunciated by Jesus in Matthew 11:28–29. First He said, "Come to Me and I will give you rest," and then He said, "You shall find rest." Well, which is it—does He give it, or do we find it? Both. By simply coming to Christ we receive rest, but there is a second rest (comparable to the life of victory) that we find only by taking His yoke and learning of Him. Rest is given but rest must be gained. There is God's side of giving and man's side of gaining.

How do we gain it? What is our part? Three things are mentioned in chapter one of Joshua.

First, *the victory is gained by faith*. Joshua was to take God at His word and start walking. And that's what faith is—acting on the word of God. "This is the victory that has overcome the world—our faith" (1 John 5:4). We exercise faith when we acknowledge that the victory has already been won for us by Christ and thank Him for it. We don't go out *to* victory—we go out *from* victory. The Christian life is lived from a platform of victory already accomplished.

> *You have no victories to win; Jesus won them all. Rely upon Him.*

Face each new day with this attitude: "Lord, thank You that every problem I meet today has already been overcome by You. Every temptation I confront today has already been put down by You." But if you meet the day hoping you can remain strong and true, determined to do your best for Jesus, you will fail miserably. *Victory isn't doing your best for Jesus; it is Jesus doing His best for you!* You have no victories to win; Jesus won them all. Rely upon Him.

Not only do we gain the victory by faith, but we gain it by *following*. God told Joshua, "Only be strong and very courageous; be careful to do according to all the law . . . do not turn from it to the right or to the left, so that you may have success wherever you go" (Josh. 1:7). Here is God's formula for success. God was actually telling Joshua that success in the forthcoming venture depended upon him. You say, "I thought it depended upon the Lord." It does, but the Lord can give us that success only as we follow His instructions.

A few years ago while on vacation, I fell down a flight of stairs and injured my ankle. I went to the emergency room of the local hospital, and as I waited for someone to help me, I noticed a sign on the wall. It said: "When all else fails, try following the directions." That was encouraging. I hoped they would try the directions first. That's what God was saying to Joshua—and to us.

The word translated "law" means "directions," and that's what God's law is—divine directions on how to put together a successful life. This will be discussed more fully in the next chapter, but for now let's get one thing clear: obedience to God's directions is an evidence of our faith, and without it there can be no victorious life.

This third point may startle you: we gain the victory by *fighting*. When the people left Egypt, God could have taken them by a direct way straight into Canaan, but He led them by a circuitous route instead. God deliberately made the journey longer. Why? The explanation is recorded in Exodus 13:17: "Now it came about when Pharaoh had let the people go, that God did not lead them by the way of the land of the Philistines, even though it was near; for God said, 'Lest the people change their minds when they see war, and they return to Egypt.'" They weren't ready to fight, and entering Canaan would take courageous fighting men, so God postponed military confrontation until they were ready.

The land of fullness is occupied by the enemy. We will not go in unopposed. Spiritual warfare is the order of the day when we move into our victory. Have you noticed that while in the wilderness, Israel didn't fight a single battle (except among themselves)? Only when they entered Canaan did they encounter warfare. That is significant.

Again, this doesn't contradict the fact that victory isn't won by our struggling and striving. Although we must fight, we fight in the power of the Lord; we are to be strong in the Lord; we are to put on the whole armor of God that we may be able to withstand all the attacks of the enemy (see Eph. 6:10–17).

But understand this: there will be conflict and confrontation. The ship of Zion is a man-of-war, not a luxury liner. At times it is easy to pray and praise the Lord; at other times it is an intense struggle. We want always to read the Bible with ease and enjoyment, but sometimes only rigid discipline makes it possible. When our flagging faith falters, our enthusiasm wanes and our bodies tire, we will need the whole armor of God to throw off the attacks of our adversary.

When you are besieged by difficulties, it means God has enrolled you in basic training, to get you ready to fight.

When a person first becomes a Christian, it often seems everything is easy for him. He witnesses, prays, reads the Bible with radiant and tireless enthusiasm. Temptations seem not to exist. God, as He did for the Israelites, is leading him in the easy way. He is not yet ready to fight. When he is suddenly besieged by difficulties, he becomes frustrated and confused, and wonders what went wrong. At this moment Satan may take advantage of his predicament and accuse him of total and terminal failure, trying to convince him that God has surely abandoned him. But God has not deserted him; He has merely enrolled the new Christian in basic training in order to get him ready to fight.

The first victory for Joshua was an easy one. No intense struggle took place at Jericho. The people simply marched thirteen times around the city, played their instruments and shouted, and the massive walls disintegrated. The ease with which Jericho was conquered was remarkable. But the other victories weren't that way. They had to fight and fight desperately. Don't assume because of Jericho that you will need only to shout a little and stage a pre-battle victory parade for the walls of spiritual opposition to flatten before you. As you mature in your victory walk, the hand-to-hand and face-to-face combat suggested by Ephesians 6 will more often be the case.

This has been a long chapter, but necessary to cover the basic truths of the life of victory. It is God's goal and gift for every believer, already accomplished by the death and resurrection of the Lord Jesus. But that doesn't mean that every Christian automatically experiences this victory. There is something for us to do. We must appropriate what God has made available.

Let me illustrate it like this: There's a water fountain in the foyer of our church. It contains cool, refreshing water for those who are thirsty. Suppose one Sunday morning after the worship hour I see you in the foyer on your knees before that fountain. With hands clasped in prayer, you're begging the fountain for water, just one little drink. But nothing happens. And nothing will happen, except that someone may carry you off in a straitjacket. You don't get water from a fountain by begging and pleading. You go up to it, bend over, push the lever, open your mouth and swallow. It's that simple.

Jesus invited all who were thirsty to come to Him and drink. He doesn't force our mouths open and pour it down us. We must do our own drinking. The fountain is waiting; come and drink.

Two

BRIDGING THE EXPERIENCE GAP

Not long ago I flew to a northern city for a speaking engagement. A man I had never seen was to meet me at the airport. But when I entered the terminal, no one approached me. Many people were waiting to meet arriving passengers, but no one headed in my direction.

After a while I was paged over the loudspeaker and asked to meet my party at the airline desk. When I got there, I immediately recognized the man waiting for me as one of those in the waiting room. I had walked right by him, and he had failed to recognize me. He apologized profusely and said, "I had your picture, but you don't look anything like it." That has happened so many times I just answer, "Well, that picture was made when I was much older."

Have you ever noticed the disturbing difference between what the Bible says we are and what we really are? It would be difficult to recognize most Christians from the description of them given in the Bible. I wonder if people would be surprised to discover that we're Christians. Might they say, "I had your picture in my Bible, but you don't look anything like it"?

Let's take a quick look at our photograph. In First John 5:4 we read, "And this is the victory that has overcome the world—our faith." I used to read that and say, "Aha, that's why I'm not overcoming the world. I don't have enough faith. If God would give me more faith, I could be victorious." Then one day I read the next verse, and it blasted that excuse into limbo: "And who is the one who overcomes the world, but he who believes that Jesus is the Son of God?"

It's not special or super-faith that overcomes the world. It's not how much faith you have, but what you have faith in. The statement is unmistakably clear. If you believe that Jesus is the Son of God, you are overcoming the world. I believed, but I wasn't overcoming the world!

Take another look at yourself. "But in all these things we overwhelmingly conquer through Him who loved us" (Rom. 8:37). The words translated "overwhelmingly conquer" are difficult to translate adequately. The Greek word conveys the idea of super- and supra-conquerors. The Christian doesn't merely conquer—he overwhelmingly conquers. Most Christians believe we'll win in the end. The Lord is going to be victorious finally. But it's going to be close! It's like a football game in which, in the last three seconds, the Christians will kick a field goal and beat the devil 17 to 14! No, that's not what Paul says—it's not the Christians 17 and the devil 14; it's the Christians 100 and the devil 0. By the way, that is not a promise; it is a statement of fact.

One more glance ought to be enough. "Whoever drinks of the water that I shall give him. shall never thirst" (John 4:14). Jesus uses a double negative for emphasis: "shall not never thirst." That's poor English but great theology. Just one drink of the water of eternal life will put a reservoir of contentment and satisfaction within the believer.

How do we cross the gulf between what we ought to be and what we are? How do we bridge the experience gap?

I see your name under the picture, but is that really you? That's sufficient to show the terrible discrepancy between portrait and practice.

So the real question is this: how do we cross the gulf between what we ought to be and what we are? How do we bridge the experience gap?

The key is the word "response." We experience what God says *of* us when we respond to what God says *to* us. As a matter of fact, all Christian living is simply a matter of response. We were saved by responding to God's offer of grace. We sought Him because He sought us. We love Him because He first loved us (1 John 4:19). "You shall be holy, for I am holy," He says (1 Pet. 1:16). And John tells us we are to walk in the light because He is in the light (1 John 1:7).

We live the Christian life the same way we received it: "As you therefore have received Christ Jesus the Lord, so walk in Him" (Col. 2:6). The Israelites got into Canaan the same way they got out of Egypt—by crossing a river. Interesting, isn't it? God's method was the same in both instances. That reveals a significant spiritual principle: God's methods never really change. We were saved by grace through faith, and we live by the same grace through the same faith. We entered the Christian life by responding in faith to Jesus Christ, and we go on in the Christian life by continuing to respond in faith to Jesus. Our response becomes the ink with which we write the history of our lives.

The Gospels provide a good example of response that led to success. One morning after Simon Peter and the other disciples had fished unsuccessfully all night, Jesus appeared and asked, "Have you caught anything?"

"No," they replied. "We have labored all night and have taken nothing."

Then Jesus told them, "Cast your nets down on the other side of the boat." Simon could have said, "Now, Master, you stick to preaching and leave the fishing to us. After all, we're professionals." Or they could have said, "We've already tried that spot," or "Our fathers fished this spot for years and taught us every trick. The fish just aren't here." Instead, Simon responded, "We have toiled all the night . . . nevertheless at thy word I will let down the net" (Luke 5:5, KJV). And their obedient response produced a bulging net.

In the first chapter of Joshua we find a threefold response to the Word of God that guarantees victory. If Joshua would make these three responses, the land that God had already given to them in promise would become theirs in experience.

1. Accept God's Promises

Someone may say, "Well, I've done that already. I accept every word in the Bible as the true, inspired Word of God." I'm sure you do, but that's not what I mean. I mean you should accept God's promises for yourself, as your very own promises, as though you were the first and only person to whom God ever spoke them.

God's promises are not limited to past saints. In God's commission to Joshua, He tells him that the promises He made to Moses were now promises to him. "Just as I have been with Moses, I will be with you; . . . you shall give this people possession of the land which I swore to their fathers to give them" (Josh. 1:5–6). The promises didn't die with Moses. God renews them with every generation. You must look at them and exclaim, "These are my promises. God promised them to me—not just to Joshua or Paul or Peter or the early church. "In Jesus Christ all the promises of God are 'Yes' and 'Amen'" (2 Cor. 1:20).

God's promises are not altered by time. Joshua was standing at the end of forty years of failure. Think of it. An entire generation had died since God had made His promise. But the years had failed to erode the promises of a God who speaks with eternity in His words. "Forever, O LORD, Thy word is settled in heaven. Thy faithfulness continues throughout all generations" (Ps. 119:89–90). Don't let a mere two thousand years separate you from God's promises!

God's promises are not affected by circumstances. Like a clap of thunder, God announced, "Moses, my servant is dead." Exit Moses—a faithful and familiar leader, a man with a face-to-face relationship with God, a trusted friend who stuck with them through every bad time.

Enter Joshua—a rookie! If the mighty Moses was unable to bring them into Canaan, who could? Surely Joshua couldn't expect to succeed where Moses failed. It was not a very encouraging situation. But God made it clear that circumstances hadn't changed His plans. How could they? He created the circumstances! God planned Moses' death, brought it about, and was in charge of the funeral Himself. Rest assured that God will never create a circumstance that conflicts with His plans, regardless of how it appears. Every circumstance, under the control of our sovereign Lord, only serves to further His redemptive purposes.

The quickest route to defeat is to concentrate on your circumstances. Thank God, victory never depends upon circumstances. Even if everyone about us fails, God is still faithful. Every adverse situation is a fresh call to believe God. Each difficulty is a new opportunity for God to demonstrate His faithfulness.

2. Abide in God's Promises

The heart of God's commission to Joshua dealt with the leader's relationship to the law of God. You can't read the first chapter of Joshua without seeing how important this was. God made it clear that the only way Joshua would succeed in his task was by knowing God's words thoroughly and keeping them faithfully.

> Be careful to do according to all the law . . .; do not turn from it to the right or to the left, so that you may have success wherever you go. This book of the law shall not depart from your mouth, but you shall meditate on it day and night, so that you may be careful to do according to all that is written in it; for then you will make your way prosperous, and then you will have success. (Josh. 1:7–8)

The word "prosper" carries the idea of making right and wise decisions. The word of God would give Joshua the ability to make the right and wise decision in every situation and thus insure success in his appointed task. We must learn this truth. Regardless of natural talent or ability, only disciplined devotion to God's Word can equip us to do God's will.

The Word of God must be placed first. In the daily life of the believer, the Bible is to occupy the place of supremacy; it is to be the law of his life. Notice that the law was set above Joshua; although he was the successor of Moses, the God-chosen leader of the people, he was to give undeviating obedience to God's command. There could not be the slightest neglect or compromise: "Do not turn from it to the right or to the left."

Our relationship to God's Word is stated by Jesus in John 14:21: "He who has My commandments and keeps them, he it is who loves Me; and he who loves Me shall be loved by My Father, and I will love him, and will disclose Myself to him."

Christ's commands are to regulate our walk, just as highway signs regulate our driving.

The key word "keep" means "to be vigilant, to keep a watchful eye upon" something. It was used of ancient mariners who kept their ships on course by vigilantly watching the stars and navigating by them. We navigate our cars the same way, keeping our eyes on the highway markers and speed-limit signs and driving accordingly. Especially do we keep a watchful eye on the rear-view mirror!

Jesus is telling us to keep a watchful eye on His commandments and conform to them. They are to regulate our walk, just as the highway signs regulate our driving.

The Word of God is to be practiced fully. First, it is to be the source of our speaking. God said to Joshua, "This book of the law shall not depart from your mouth" (Josh. 1:8). The law was to direct his speech and dominate his conversation. Peter said, "Whoever speaks, let him speak, as it were, the utterances of God" (1 Pet. 4:11).

Writing to the Ephesians, Paul said, "Let no unwholesome word proceed from your mouth, but only such a word as is good for edification according to the need of the moment, that it may give grace to those who hear" (Eph. 4:29). And to the Colossians he wrote, "Let your speech always be with grace, seasoned, as it were, with salt, so that you may know how you should respond to each person" (Col. 4:6).

John Bunyan was converted as a result of overhearing a conversation among several women. If someone eavesdropped on you, would your conversation point him to Christ?

Second, the Word of God is to be the subject of our thinking. "You shall meditate on it day and night," God commanded Joshua. And significantly, it was this meditating on the Word of God that would enable him to obey all that was written in it (Josh. 1:8).

This is the same word that appears in Psalm 1:2: "But his delight is in the law of the LORD, and in His law he meditates day and night." Verse 3 reveals the result of such delightful meditation: "And he will be like a tree firmly planted by streams of water, which yields its fruit in its season, and its leaf does not wither; and in whatever he does, he prospers."

That's exactly what God said to Joshua. Almost gives you the idea God is trying to tell us something, doesn't it? Well, He is. He is trying to tell us that meditating on the Word of God is the secret of spiritual prosperity!

The Hebrew word translated "meditate" has the overtones of "humming." A famous popular singer was asked why he was always humming. He answered that humming kept his vocal cords warmed up and ready to perform at a moment's notice. And our constant humming of the Word, meditating on it day and night, will keep us warmed up and ready to obey at a moment's notice. The Word of God is to be like a tune you can't get out of your head; it is to permeate your life and be absorbed into your system. Then and only then will you be able to act wisely. When you encounter a situation you don't know how to handle, God will be able to give you unbelievable wisdom, because you have been abiding in His Word.

3. Act on God's Promises

I met a man recently who said he had been having a regular time of Bible study and prayer, and had even been memorizing Scripture. "But," he complained, "it hasn't made any difference." After talking with him awhile, I discovered he lacked one thing: he had not been acting on what he learned. It's not enough to read your Bible regularly, memorize it and meditate on it; you must obey it. The purpose of meditation, as we have seen, is obedience: "meditate on it day and night, so that you may be careful to do according to all that is written in it; for then . . . you will have success" (Josh. 1:8).

Reading the Bible will give you knowledge *about* God; obeying the Bible will give you knowledge *of* God. Many Christians know a lot about God but do not know God Himself in a personal and intimate fellowship. It is when you begin doing what you have been reading that your life begins changing. God doesn't give us scriptural knowledge for information's sake; He isn't interested in satisfying our curiosity or scratching our intellectual itch. God is interested in our obedience. And that's the purpose of all revelation. "Thy word have I treasured in my mind that I might amaze my friends" is the attitude of many who aren't the least bit interested in hiding it in their hearts that they might not sin against God (Ps. 119:11).

Obedience is cooperation with God. God had already given the land, but Joshua had to walk across it before he received it. And he was given only as much as he walked across. The same is true for us. God gives you only as much as you are willing to walk across in obedience.

Obedience is confidence in God. It is confidence in His promise. "I have given it to you," God said. I have made a marvelous discovery. God never asks you to do something without giving you the power to do it. Our obedience is simply saying amen to God's promise. Joshua could take the land because God had already given it to him. This means that disobedience is an assault on the character of God; it is saying, "God, You can't be trusted." On the other hand, obedience is saying, "God, I trust You, and to prove my trust I'm going to do everything You tell me."

But more than this, obedience is confidence in His presence. Listen to verse 9: "Have I not commanded you? Be strong and courageous! Do not tremble or be dismayed, for the LORD your God is with you wherever you go." It is His presence that gives you the courage to obey, even when faced with unbelievable problems and insurmountable obstacles. And He will go with you even more closely than He went with Joshua, because He actually lives within you through His Holy Spirit.

Friend, you hold the key to the door of victory. The key is your response to the promises of God. Use it, and you will unlock the vault to all of heaven's resources.

Three

GETTING READY TO GO

As a kid I loved it when the family talked about taking a trip. I remember Dad bringing home road maps of the states we wanted to visit, and in the evening we would spread them on the floor and choose the easiest route and the best places to stop. Of course, like most families, we talked more than we traveled. But occasionally the hoped-for opportunity would come and we'd be off!

Do you know how I knew we were actually going? When Mom made preparations to leave. Getting ready to go was the sign—and the best part of the trip! It was also the hardest and most important, often taking longer than the trip itself.

It's the same in the spiritual realm. Preparation is an act of faith. If we really believe God is going to do something, we get ready for it. When we pray for rain, we ought to carry an umbrella. In my own spiritual pilgrimage, I am discovering that God gives me only what I am prepared to receive.

After God spoke to Joshua, the new leader came away convinced God would go with them and give them the land. He was so certain of this that he ordered the people to get ready for immediate action. God had spoken and preparation was the evidence of their faith in that spoken word. The Bible says:

Most Christians exist on a desert diet—just enough to keep tham alive. To move into the land of promise, you must upgrade your diet and increase your intake.

> Then Joshua commanded the officers of the people, saying, "Pass through the midst of the camp and command the people, saying, 'Prepare provisions for yourselves, for within three days you are to cross this Jordan, to go in to possess the land which the LORD your God is giving you, to possess it.' . . . "Consecrate yourselves, for tomorrow the LORD will do wonders among you." (Josh. 1:10–11; 3:5)

It is the prepared people who possess the land; therefore, we need to examine the preparations required for the trip into Canaan.

A New Diet

"Prepare provisions," God said. That's interesting. Here is an entire nation, possibly three million people, about to cross a flooding river, and what is the first thing they are to prepare? A bridge? That would seem reasonable. Boats, at least. But without a bridge or a boat in sight, God told them to prepare—*bread.*

During the wilderness years God provided manna to eat. Now, if you're stranded in a desert with no other food, manna is all right, but it has been highly overrated in sermons and songs. Manna was a coarse, dry, hard bread—not steak and potatoes. It could sustain but not satisfy. Get this: the diet that was adequate to maintain life in the desert would not nourish combat troops conquering and settling a new land.

Most of the Christians I know exist on a desert diet—just enough to keep them alive. But if you want to move into the land of promise and experience daily victory you must upgrade your diet and increase your intake.

I'm talking about your personal worship time with the Lord in prayer and the Word. Much has been said about this already because I am convinced that this is the single most important factor in consistent Christian living. How much time have you spent today alone with God on your knees before an open Bible? If you're serious about a victorious life, then determine right now that, whatever the cost or sacrifice, you will establish a daily time with God in prayer and Bible study. The strength and stamina you have in the conflicts of life will be determined by the quality of nourishment you receive from the Lord.

A New Delay

This part of their preparation is even more surprising than the first. There would be a three-day delay. "Lord, why this delay?" I can imagine the Israelites saying. "We've been delayed forty years already and now we're ready to go." But God said, "Wait."

One of the things I've learned about God is that He never hurries. The toughest thing I have to do is wait, and I hate it. We Americans are accustomed to instant gratification: instant credit, instant comfort and instant coffee. Our cry is, "Lord, give me patience— right now!" But God never wastes time, and every delay plays an important role in His plan.

God used the delay to accomplish three things. First, it was a time of *observation.* The people had to camp on the banks of the Jordan for three days—and what did they do during that time? They watched the swollen river surging over its banks. "We're going to cross *that*?" they must have whispered to one another. "But there's no bridge, no boats? It can't be done!" That's the point exactly. God was letting the impossibility of the task sink into their minds.

Has God ever dealt with you that way? He has with me. Many times He has plopped me down beside the Jordan of my life and forced me to look at it. The longer I looked, the more impossible the situation became. I would cry out for deliverance, wondering how God could love me and yet refuse to remove the problem. I could see no boat, no bridges, no way of getting through the situation. After a while I would know that apart from God there was no solution. When we are convinced that only God can get it all together, then we're ready to move.

The delay was also a time of *confrontation*. Forty years earlier, twelve spies were sent out from Kadesh-barnea. It was their faithless report, blurted out in front of all the people, that caused them to turn back and forfeit the land. This time Joshua sent out two spies, who spent these three days scouting the land. Their report, brought privately to Joshua, declared that God was surely with them—all the inhabitants of the country were terrified of them. God used the waiting period to confirm His promise.

During those frustrating delays, if we keep our eyes and ears attuned to God, He will give us one evidence after another that He is capable of handling our situation.

The delay was also a time of *separation*. While Moses was still alive, the tribes of Reuben and Gad and the half-tribe of Manasseh became enchanted with the wilderness close to the Jordan River. It was fertile land and they wanted to settle down there. They preferred the wilderness. Angrily, Moses said, "Oh, so you want to let your brothers go on and fight alone for the land God has given to all of us. Well, you can stay here if you want, but first you must go over and fight with the rest of us." And they agreed. In verses 12 through 18 of chapter 1, Joshua honored the decision made by Moses and those tribes.

That incident is packed with spiritual instruction. God lets us choose the level of our Christian experience. He forces no one to enter into victory. If the wilderness is what you want, the wilderness is what you will get.

The descendants of those tribes are found in every church. They do their share of the fighting but always return to their spiritual wilderness, refusing to live in the victory Christ has won for them. They help with the budget, the building program, the Bible school; they support the pastor and faithfully attend the worship services, but when twelve noon strikes, they tuck their Bibles under their arms and plod wearily back to a barren and defeated life.

The Bible commands us to set ourselves apart from the filthiness of the world; this is a "must" for the life of victory.

The tragic conclusion to the story is that these two-and-a-half tribes were the first to be conquered and carried into captivity when the Assyrians attacked in later years. When the real testing comes, the first to falter and fail are those who choose to live on the wrong side of Jordan.

A New Dedication

After the period of waiting, Joshua told the people to consecrate themselves. The last time they had heard this command was when Moses went up to the mountain to receive the law from God (see Exod. 19:10–11). He told the people to consecrate themselves so they would be ready to hear God's words upon his return. This was an old dedication; a lot had happened since then, and they had long since been unfaithful. Now God was about to do something new, and they needed a new dedication.

Consecrate means "to purify, to sanctify, to make something holy by setting it apart for special use." There is a sense in which God sanctifies us and another sense in which we sanctify ourselves.

By virtue of our salvation, we are all sanctified, set apart for God's special use; every Christian is a saint. But the Bible also commands us to purify ourselves (1 John 3:3), to set ourselves apart from the filthiness of the world; and this is a "must" for the life of victory.

We must be willing to deal with our sins—confess and forsake them—and allow God to cleanse us from all unrighteousness (1 John 1:9). Just a casual reading of Joshua 7 reveals the devastating effects of hidden sin in the life of one believer. God demands holiness.

We must be holy in our public life. Our activities are to be pure. Exodus 19 shows that this process of purification required that the people wash their garments: "The LORD also said to Moses, 'Go to the people and consecrate them today and tomorrow, and let them wash their garments'" (Exod. 19:10). The garments, seen by all, were to be spotless. We are to present to the world a clean life; our activities must be above reproach.

We must be holy in our private life. Our affections are to be pure. This was symbolized in the purification rite by marital abstinence for a period of time. "And he said to the people, 'Be ready for the third day; do not go near a woman'" (Exod. 19:15). This indicated a complete dedication to the Lord in the most intimate affairs. When we get down to business with God, our private lives will be characterized by holiness. Let me suggest you pray through Psalm 139, especially the last two verses: "Search me, O God, and know my heart; try me and know my anxious thoughts; and see if there be any hurtful way in me, and lead me in the everlasting way" (Ps. 139:23–24).

It might be good to stop at this point and catch up with yourself. Think about what you've read so far. Are you weary of the wilderness? Does your heart cry out for the "much more" of Christ? Above everything else in the world, do you want to know Christ in all His fullness? Are you ready to let Jesus, our Joshua, lead you into the promised land? If so, then consecrate yourself; get ready, for the Lord is ready to do wonders in your life.

Four

HARK, THE ARK!

It's sobering to realize that one day can alter your entire life. In just twenty-four hours your world, with its hopes and plans, can be reduced to ashes—or it can be wondrously transformed beyond your wildest expectations. The direction of world history has often been determined by the events of a single day.

It was that way with Israel. In one day they moved out of forty years of failure and reproach into the greatest era of their history. A nation flat on its back sprang to its feet and marched victoriously into a new land.

What was special about that day? What was the key to their triumph? This isn't an idle question simply to satisfy historical curiosity. Remember that the events of that day were recorded as examples to us. God's methods, like Himself, do not change, and to discover the key to Israel's victory is to discover the key to our own.

The third chapter of Joshua relates the happenings of that day. A close study shows that the main figure in the drama was the ark of the covenant. It is mentioned ten times.

> And they commanded the people, saying, "When you see the ark of the covenant of the LORD your God with the Levitical priests carrying it, then you shall set out from your place and go after it . . . And it shall come about when the soles of the feet of the priests who carry the ark of the LORD, the Lord of all the earth, shall rest in the waters of the Jordan, the waters of the Jordan shall be cut off. . . ." And the priests who carried the ark of the covenant of the LORD stood firm on dry ground in the middle of the Jordan while all Israel crossed on dry ground, until all the nation had finished crossing the Jordan. (Josh. 3:3, 13, 17)

It isn't the possession of Christ but the position of Christ that counts. Only when Christ is enthroned as Lord and Leader can we experience fullness.

Without question, the ark was the key to their victory. But what was different about it on that day? They had possessed the ark, made according to God's instructions, since Moses met God on Mount Sinai. During the long, bitter years of wandering the ark had been in their midst, but there had been no victory.

But now, on this day, something had changed. Do you know what it was? *The position of the ark.* Before, the ark had been in the *midst* of the Israelites; now it was at their head. The ark had always gone with the people but now the people were to go with the ark. God commanded them not to move until they saw the ark. As it came into view, they were to follow it; it was to be kept in sight all the time. When the priests, *carrying the ark*, stepped into the swollen river, the waters halted and rose in a heap. And while the priests, still *carrying the ark*, stood in the middle, the entire nation walked across on dry ground. It was the ark!

The Old Testament ark was a picture of our Lord Jesus Christ. He is our Ark of the New Covenant. We have possessed Him since the day of our salvation, but possession alone doesn't guarantee victory. It isn't the *possession* of Christ but the *position* of Christ that counts.

The difference between the victorious Christian and the defeated Christian is not in what they possess. God doesn't play favorites, giving one believer a larger portion of His Spirit than He gives another. We are all complete in Christ (Col. 2:9). The difference lies in the position the possession occupies in each life. Only when Christ is enthroned as Lord and Leader can we experience His fullness.

It's one thing to accept the lordship of Christ as an article of faith and quite another to accept it as a practical, governing force in our lives. Is He Lord? Does He control your actions, attitudes and affections? Is He Lord at home, at school, at work?

J. Hudson Taylor was correct when He said that Christ is either Lord of all or not Lord at all. He is Lord of everything or not Lord of anything. Simply stated, the key to the victorious Christian life is the enthroning of Jesus Christ as Lord.

As Lord, Christ Is the Door to Our Unclaimed Possessions

The land of Canaan had belonged to Israel for years, but they had never set foot in it until they had followed the ark across the Jordan River. The ark was the door to their unclaimed possessions and unexperienced blessings.

What I'm going to say now is the most important part of the book. The victorious life is not an experience or a formula or a certain way of behaving—it is a Person. That person is Jesus Christ; He is the victorious life. Triumphant living isn't getting things from Christ; it is realizing we already have all things in Christ. Jesus said, "I am the door" to abundant life (John 10:9–10). The abundant life is the life of Jesus residing, reigning and released in the believer.

My favorite passage is Colossians 2:9–10: "For in Him all the fullness of Deity dwells in bodily form, and in Him you have been made complete." What can you add to completeness? When God gave us Christ, He gave us everything, for all the fullness of the Godhead abides in Him. After we've been in heaven a million years, we'll possess no more of God than we do right now. Only the circumstances of that possession will be different.

Think of it like this: Jesus doesn't give peace; He is our Peace (Eph. 2:14). He doesn't give knowledge; He is our Knowledge (Col. 2:3). He doesn't give wisdom and righteousness and sanctification and redemption; He is all these things Himself (1 Cor. 1:30). If we're hungry, He is the Bread of Life; if we're thirsty, He is the Fountain of Living Water; if we're lost, He is the Way; if we're blind, He is the Light of the World; if we're lonely, He is the Friend that sticketh closer than a brother; if we're dying, He is the Resurrection and the Life.

He's the Way and what we find at the end of the Way. He is the Door and what we find on the other side of the Door. He is the Fountain and the Water that flows from the Fountain. He is the cause of His own effect and the effect of His own cause; He is the means and the end. He is God's everything to the believer!

My wife has given birth to three children. I suppose the first thing mothers all over the world do the first time they hold their baby is check to see if they are all there! You know—all the standard equipment: ten fingers, ten toes, two ears, one mouth. At birth God gave our three children everything they would ever need to live physically. Lying helpless in the crib, they didn't know what to do with their feet—they didn't even know they had feet.

When it came time for them to walk, we didn't have to take them to the hospital and tell the doctor to put on their legs. Legs are standard equipment on babies, God's birthday gift to them, even though at the time they can't use them. But the day came when our children discovered that those two things they had been dragging behind them would support them and, if placed one in front of the other, would take them where mother said not to go. A whole new world opened up and life was never the same again—for them or their mother! *Physical growth is discovering what you received at birth and learning to use it.*

When we learn to appropriate all Christ is for all we need, life is never again the same.

Likewise, at my spiritual birth God gave me everything I would ever need to live spiritually—Jesus Christ. *And spiritual growth is discovering what God gave me at salvation and learning to appropriate it.* Like the baby who learns to walk, when we discover we are complete in Christ and learn to appropriate all He is for all we need, life is never again the same.

As Lord, Jesus Directs Us over Uncharted Paths

"When you see the ark . . . then you shall set out from your place and go after it. However, there shall be between you and it a distance of about 2,000 cubits by measure. Do not come near it, that you may know the way by which you shall go, for you have not passed this way before" (Josh. 3:3–4).

It has always been God's pattern to lead His people where they have never been. He called Abraham into a far country—He didn't even tell him what country. Joseph went from a rural society into slavery and finally to the ruling seat of a sophisticated culture. Paul, an elite Jew, became a missionary to the despised Gentiles.

Joshua was confronted with a Herculean task— an untried leader guiding an unsettled people into an unknown country. And if that wasn't enough, the first thing they must do is ford an unfordable river. How? God's directions were simple: "Just keep your eye on the ark."

"You have not passed this way before." I don't know of a phrase that better depicts the venture of daily living. No one knows what a day may bring. Each day is unexplored territory. No one has ever lived it before. Every person is an amateur. Sometimes it's like walking barefoot through snake-infested grass at night without a flashlight. This is one of the things that makes life such a terrifying undertaking to so many people.

But we really don't need to know where we're headed or how we'll get there—we need only to watch for the Ark and go after it. Years ago I heard an old preacher say, "Don't start down the road till you see Jesus." That's what God was saying to Joshua.

Keeping our eyes on Jesus means we depend upon Him. We count on His ability, not our inability. The overwhelming lesson of the Jordan crossing is that the power of God negates the problems of man.

Keeping our eyes on Jesus also means we focus our attention on Him and not on the hindrances. And that's the main reason God leads us through unknown territory—He is really leading us to Himself. If He had revealed to Abraham the location of the far country, Abraham would have fixed his eyes on the destination and would have determined for himself when he had traveled far enough. Since God alone knew the destination, Abraham had to keep his eyes on God—which is where God wanted them. Of course, we prefer to know all the details of the trip, every hill and curve and turn, but God prefers we know how to follow Him. Perhaps this will unravel the mystery of why God is keeping you in the dark about a certain situation. He may be using it to draw you into a deeper and more intimate fellowship with Himself.

This makes it necessary that nothing block our view of Him. God told Israel to keep the ark in front of them at a distance of about four-and-a-half football fields "that you may know the way by which you shall go." In other words, the ark was to be clearly visible at all times; nothing was to come between it and the people.

Christ doesn't elevate us above our problems; He's a path through them.

Imagine what would have happened if the people had jammed around the ark. It would have disappeared in the crowd and every Israelite, without knowing it, would have ended up following the person in front of him. Talk about the blind leading the blind! I can picture a gang of them winding up in some dead-end wasteland, scratching their heads in bewilderment and hurling accusations at one another:

"I was following you! I thought you were following the ark."

"Not me. I was following him. I thought he was following it."

"Not me. I haven't seen the thing for days. I was following him. He acted like he knew where he was going."

That very thing is happening today among believers. No wonder so few ever make it to the promised land.

As Lord, Jesus Delivers Us from Unconquerable Problems

While at a youth conference, I heard someone sing, "Christ is a Bridge Over Troubled Waters." That's a beautiful sentiment, but untrue. Many seem to think that the victorious life is a vaccine against problems. Neither the life of Jesus nor the lives of the disciples bear this out. Christ doesn't elevate us above problems. He isn't a bridge over troubled waters, but He is a path through them.

All of us must pass through troubled waters. Not a single Israelite was exempt from the crossing; each one had to pass through the flood. I have no doubt that many trembled as they hurried by the towering mountain of water poised over them. In the middle of your Jordan, it doesn't matter that others have been there and safely reached the opposite side; you feel as though you're the only one who has stood in that place. I know; I've been there.

But that's where the ark is! Thank God, right in the middle of your Jordan with that menacing wall of water frowning upon you, you find the Ark. What a relief! Surely the water won't crash down upon the Ark. While it's there, you're safe. I don't think you ever know how real Jesus can be until you meet Him in the middle of an unconquerable problem. And that is preparation for greater battles. For when you encounter Him in your raging torrent, you know for sure He can manage a land full of giants.

I heard of a Sunday school teacher who asked her class of small girls if one of them could quote the 23rd Psalm. A girl timidly raised her hand and said she could. She stood in front of the class and said, "The Lord is my shepherd. That's all I want."

I think she quoted it correctly. For when the Shepherd is your Lord, He becomes everything you want—that is the victorious life.

Five

PLUGGING INTO THE POWER

It was going to be a great Christmas. I could hardly wait until the kids saw all the neat toys waiting under the tree—games that lit up and buzzed, tanks that fired plastic missiles, cars that raced on a winding track. But as they eagerly ripped open the packages, I noticed for the first time something printed on the cartons: "Batteries Not Included." *Batteries!* It was exciting all right, sitting around staring at immobile tanks and stalled race cars and ignoring little voices that kept repeating, "Daddy, this won't work."

Spiritually, that has been the frustrating experience of many Christians. Time and again, they have had everything but the power. And you might as well try to swim without water as to try to live the Christian life without God's power. If the biblical account of entering Canaan teaches anything, it is that victory demands the release of God's power in our behalf. Knowing how to plug into this power is absolutely essential.

God's power is always flowing. If at times it seems that God is idle, it is only because we have stepped out of the stream. In this chapter and the next, we will discuss the streams in which the power of God flows.

God's Power Flows in the Stream of His Purpose

God uses His power to accomplish His purposes. It is never released simply to indulge our carnal cravings or to bail us out of a spot He didn't lead us into. God is no show-off; He isn't running a sideshow for the amusement of miracle-mongers. I was about ten years old when I saw the original *The King of Kings* classic by Cecil B. De Mille. The scene where Jesus stands before Herod brought me to the edge of my seat. Herod kept asking Jesus to perform a miracle, and Jesus wouldn't even answer the old reprobate. As I sat there in the darkness, I wanted to jump up and shout, "Do it, Jesus! Work a miracle. Show 'em who You are!" But He didn't. That was not the stream of His purpose.

God has a purpose, a plan for every life, and we must find and fit into that purpose.

We have a tendency to treat God like a glorified butler, or a genie who, when we rub our prayer lamp, materializes to grant our every wish. But He is not our servant; He is the Lord of life who makes plans and executes them. It isn't His concern to accomplish our goals, no matter how right they seem to us. The exercise of His power is reserved exclusively for the accomplishment of His purpose. But if we let Him, He will sweep us up in the mainstream of His purpose. Then we will know His power. God has a purpose, a plan for every life, and we must find and fit into that purpose. Let's look at three characteristics of His plan for our lives.

It is an *eternal* purpose. Just as God had long centuries before planned for Israel to occupy Canaan, so God in eternity past drew up a design for our life. We are God's "workmanship" created to do the good works He planned for each of us before the foundation of the world (Eph. 2:10). Isn't that a staggering thought! Before I was born, before even the worlds were formed, God singled me out and created a custom-made plan for my life. True success in life is knowing what God created you to do and doing it.

Paul was captivated by the knowledge that God had chosen him before he was born. On the Damascus road he met the living Christ, and as God's purpose began to unfold, he fitted himself into it. Jeremiah was also conscious of God's eternal plan. He first argued with the Lord about his credentials and abilities until God revealed that before he was born, God had known him and chosen him for a specific task.

This perfect plan may include difficulties with which He intends us to live. With the three Hebrew children thrown into the fiery furnace, we must be able to say,

"Our God is able to deliver us. But if He chooses not to, that will be all right" (see Dan. 3:17–18). The purpose of God rises above every other consideration.

God's purpose for our life is an *essential* purpose. It is essential to the fulfillment of our destiny. To miss God's purpose is to waste our life in aimless wandering. God tuned all things to magnify His name. You were created to be a showcase for His glory.

It is essential to our well-being. Our wholeness and happiness depend on our moving toward the goal for which we were created. Diverting our energies toward any other goal drains us of all effectiveness and turns us into misfits in a universe tuned to the glory of God. It's like playing a sensitive stereo recording of a complex symphony on a child's toy record player. The music would be a miserable facsimile of what it was intended to be. And if the record could feel, it would be frustrated and disappointed with the results.

As Paul stormed toward Damascus to imprison those who worshiped Christ, the Lord Jesus appeared to him in a blinding light and said, "Paul, it is painful to kick against the goads." A goad was a sharp, pointed stick used to keep oxen moving in the right direction. It was painful for the ox, trying to go his own way, to kick at the goad instead of yielding to its prodding. Jesus said, "Paul, why are you fighting against me? You're only hurting yourself." I'm sure all of us have scars caused by the goads. Oxen have sense enough to stop kicking— sometimes men do not.

Finally, the purpose of God is an *exciting* purpose. I doubt that a single Israelite died of boredom. I know that none of the apostles did. As they plunged forward in God's purpose, He continued to do wonders among them. Every Christian who walks with God will find wonders unfolding each day. Pretty soon you'll find yourself starting every day saying, "Well, Lord, what's it to be today?" Maybe it will be the contentment of a quiet stroll, perhaps the turbulence of a stormy battle or the satisfaction of giving yourself in service to one in need.

Moving in the stream of God's purpose is exciting. It's thrilling to see the obstacles collapse like eggshells as God guides you with His presence and guards you with His power. When Paul was sailing to Rome, the ship was engulfed in a great storm. Frantically, the sailors began to jettison the cargo, but the storm intensified, and it seemed certain that the ship and all its passengers would be lost.

That night Paul held a private prayer meeting, and the next morning he stood in the midst of his terrified shipmates and said, "Cheer up!" (Christians sometimes say pretty strange things.) He told them that as he was praying an angel from God assured him he would live to preach the gospel at Rome; therefore, the storm would pass without the loss of any life, only the loss of the ship (Acts 27:14–44). God's *eternal* plan called for Paul to proclaim the gospel message in Rome. It was *essential* to God, to Rome and to Paul. And it was *exciting*, to say the least. You and I will find it so in our lives if we're willing to be carried by the current of God's purpose.

God's Power Flows in the Stream of His Timing

It's clear from the third chapter of Joshua that a timetable arranged by the Lord was being followed. As this heavenly schedule was kept, the people fitted into the countdown of the Lord. Understanding the principle of God's timing is indispensable if God's power is to be released. Because they fail to recognize this, many Christians have their permanent residence in "Panic Palace" at the corner of "Fretful Avenue" and "Worry-Yourself-Sick Boulevard."

During a difficult and trying time in our lives, a friend gave us a wall clock with this inscription in large letters: "God's Timing Is Always Perfect." That clock hangs on our kitchen wall and greets us every morning with its reassuring message. God's timing is always perfect. He's never late. Of course, He's never early, either, but He is always right on time.

You can do the right thing at the wrong time. Moses, for instance, knew God would deliver His people from the bondage of Egypt. Escaping Pharaoh's massacre of Hebrew infants, and having been sheltered in the heart of the king's household, he figured he had been chosen to effect this deliverance. And he figured correctly. But he got ahead of God and started the campaign by killing an Egyptian bully. I guess he thought he could do the job by killing off all the Egyptians one at a time. He failed to calculate how long it would take by that method or how hot things would get when the Egyptian police discovered the murder. The result was that Moses lost the confidence of his own people (no one trusts a man who works in the energy of the flesh) and spent the next forty years hiding in the desert. When God was ready, the people were taken out in one night.

Abraham missed God's timing too. God promised him and Sarah a son who would be the beginning of a mighty nation. The years passed, but the promise remained unfulfilled. Fearing that old age would cancel the promise of God, Abraham had a son by his wife's servant girl (a perfectly legal way to do things in those days). But man can never bring to pass the purposes of God, and it is a foolish and dangerous thing to try. Nothing but disaster resulted from Abraham's effort to "help God out."

One of God's most difficult tasks is teaching us to wait.

Time spent waiting on God is never wasted. We waste time when we refuse to wait upon the Lord and take matters into our own hands. Sometimes the work of God is set back for years as a consequence of our bungling attempts. One of God's most difficult tasks is teaching us to wait. One day a friend of Phillips Brooks, a great preacher of another generation, called on him and found him impatiently pacing the floor. He asked what the trouble was. With flashing eyes Dr. Brooks exclaimed, "The trouble is that I am in a hurry and God is not!"

Jesus' life exhibits the perfect timing of God. The Bible tells us that "when the fulness of the time came, God sent forth His Son" (Gal. 4:4). God kept Jesus practically hidden for thirty years before launching Him on His public ministry. If we had been in charge of S.O.W. (Save Our World) when Jesus showed up in the temple at the age of 12, we would have immediately put Him on the evangelistic circuit.

"The world is going to hell," we would have argued. "You're wasting your time in that carpenter's shop." But God took thirty years to prepare Jesus for a three-year ministry. God's timing was illustrated by Jesus' statement, "my hour has not yet come," which is repeated throughout the Gospels. Several times the Jews tried to kill Him, but could not because "His hour was not yet come." He always slipped easily away until God said, "Now."

On two notable occasions Jesus' timing must have seemed like criminal delay to the others involved. One was on His way to the bedside of a desperately ill child. He suddenly stopped to talk with a woman about her illness and her many trips to the doctor (and you know how long that can take!). Just as He was about to resume His journey, a servant rushed up to the girl's father and told him the child was dead.

Another time, Lazarus was ill, and Mary and Martha, his sisters, sent for Jesus. He purposely delayed a few more days before going to them. When He finally reached them, Lazarus was dead, and the sisters rebuked Him saying, "If you had been here, our brother would not have died."

In both situations Jesus' delays meant death. If Jesus had followed man's timing, it would have saved much grief and anxiety, but following God's timing bestowed other benefits and even greater joy. God always has His reasons. These two incidents, as well as the crossing of Jordan, show us three reasons for divine delays.

God's delays *display our helplessness*. The delay in crossing the Jordan convinced the people that only God could take them to the other side. As long as Jairus' daughter was sick, there was still hope. When she died, all hope vanished. At the time Jesus received word of Lazarus' condition, there was still a chance. When Jesus arrived, the brother had been in the tomb four days.

God often waits until things are absolutely hopeless in our lives too. We must be completely convinced that God's power alone can deliver us.

God's delays *deepen our faith*. In both instances of Jesus' delay, the level of trust in Him was lifted. They already trusted Him to heal, but He showed them they could trust Him for even more—the restoration of life. When there was no longer any human reason to believe, Jesus urged them to believe anyway. Real faith operates when we have nothing to cling to but the bare promise of God. God uses delays to create situations in which, like muscles, our faith is exercised. Just as exercise strengthens our physical muscles, so the exercise of faith strengthens our spiritual muscles. Without a program of exercise imposed upon us through delay, we would never grow stronger.

God's delays *demonstrate His glory*. Which glorifies God more—healing a sick man or raising a dead man? Leading you across a calm and shallow Jordan or making a dry path through a raging one? This is why God lets things get blacker: it causes His glory to stand out more clearly. It must be obvious that He has done it. Then He will be seen as unsurpassingly glorious, and His people will praise Him in the temple and trust Him in trouble.

If God is to release His power in your life, you must fling yourself wholeheartedly into the stream of His purpose and wait with steadfast expectancy for Him to do His work.

Six

Every Christian Must

A car may have a tankful of gasoline, but unless the fuel is ignited, it won't move an inch. I know many Christians whose tanks are full, but they are still stalled between the Red Sea and the Jordan River. For years I was puzzled by members of my church who knew the Bible like scholars, could hear a sin drop a mile away, traveled hundreds of miles to attend Bible conferences, but whose lives lacked the plus of Christlikeness. In spite of all their knowledge and activity, there was no sign of spiritual maturity; love, joy, peace and the other characteristics of a spiritual life were conspicuously absent. They had plenty of fuel—high-octane stuff at that—but no spark to ignite it.

The purpose and timing of God constitute the fuel of victory in the Christian life. And the spark that ignites it, releasing it as a practical and powerful force in the life, is *obedience*. God's power flows in the stream of our obedience.

These first two conditions for experiencing God's power—His purpose and timing—are God's business alone. They are His responsibility entirely. God never consults with us about either His purpose or His schedule. But obedience is our responsibility. Even though the ability to obey comes from God, we, and we alone, are accountable for obedience. When the time is right, God reveals to us His purpose, then says, "Now it's your move." And at that moment everything hinges upon our obedience. We dealt with obedience in chapter 2. In this chapter I want to look more deeply into the nature of it.

Why couldn't the Israelites enter the Promised Land—because of disobedience or unbelief? It was both.

What motivates us to obey God—what is its basis? The record of the Jordan crossing is a testimony to the unquestioning and unhesitating obedience of Joshua. Under such adverse and pessimistic circumstances, how was he able to obey so admirably? The answer is actually simple: he trusted God. Obedience is the evidence and expression of our faith in God. Obedience is faith turned inside out. Faith is the seed, and obedience is the flower that springs from it. Faith is the root; obedience is the fruit. There is a very interesting passage of Scripture in Hebrews three. The inspired author is recounting Israel's failure to enter into Canaan. "And to whom did He swear that they should not enter His rest, but to those who were disobedient? And so we see that they were not able to enter because of unbelief" (Heb. 3:18–19).

In verse 18 he says they couldn't enter because of disobedience; in verse 19 he says unbelief was the cause. Well, which was it—disobedience or unbelief? It was both. For obedience and faith are two sides of the same coin. You act on what you believe, and you obey whom you trust. If you were to ask the Sunday morning worshipers if they believe the Bible from cover to cover, probably all would say they do. Yet the truth is you believe only as much of the Bible as you are obeying! What you don't obey, you don't believe.

Not long ago a friend called on the phone and asked me, "Will you do me a favor?"

"What is it?" I asked.

"Hey, come on," he said. "Will you do me a favor? "

"Tell me what it is first."

"What's the matter? Don't you trust me?"

I laughed and said, "Nope."

Get the point? I was joking with him, of course, but if I really trusted him, I wouldn't be afraid to commit myself to him. If we are reluctant to give unquestioning obedience to God, it is because we really don't trust Him.

That leads to another question: if obedience comes from trust, where does trust come from? And the answer is—knowledge. You won't obey someone you don't trust, and you can't trust someone you don't know. So here is the spiritual equation for obedience: *knowledge of God equals faith in God equals obedience to God.*

When Joshua unfolded God's plan to the people, a plan that called for bold and resolute obedience, he made several references to the character of the God who was commanding them. He was saying, "Don't be afraid to do what God tells you; you can trust Him."

He is the Lord of all the earth. This title appears in verse 11 of chapter 3: "Behold, the ark of the covenant of the Lord of all the earth," and again in verse 13: "And it shall come about when the soles of the feet of the priests who carry the ark of the LORD, the Lord of all the earth . . ." This phrase indicates the sovereign authority of God. He is the supreme ruler of the whole earth; therefore, it is His right to command. He has the right to command not only me but also nature, for He is the Lord of all the earth. He is Lord of the Jordan as well as Lord of the Jews. Praise God, if He commands you to walk across Jordan, He will command the Jordan to get out of your way!

He is the living God. "And Joshua said, 'By this you shall know that the living God is among you, and that He will assuredly dispossess from before you the Canaanite . . ." (Josh. 3:10). Because He is a living God, He is aware of our circumstances. He is not an unfeeling, uncaring God of wood or stone, but a living God who in all our affliction is afflicted too.

Not only is He aware of our circumstances; He is active in them. The evidence that He is living, Joshua said, is that He will make our enemies flee from us. "Resist the devil and he will flee from you," James 4:7 declares. A beautiful picture of God's activity on our behalf appears in chapter 5 of Joshua. Right before the battle of Jericho, Joshua meets a man standing in his path with a sword in his hand. Joshua goes up to him and asks, "Are you on our side or theirs?" And the man answers, "Neither. I have come as captain of the host of the Lord." The man, who I believe was the Lord Jesus in a preincarnation appearance, was actually saying, "I haven't come to take sides—I have come to take over!"

"When the enemy shall come in like a flood, the Spirit of the LORD shall lift up a standard against him" (Isa. 59:19, KJV).

He is a covenant God. The ark is described as the "ark of the covenant" seven times in chapter 3. Obviously this phrase held a special significance to the Israelites. A covenant is an agreement, a binding contract. The Lord of the earth entered into a contract with Israel in which He committed Himself to them as their God to act in their behalf. The covenant was originally made with Abraham and sealed by blood. Since the covenant was a contract between two parties with mutual responsibilities, the law was given to spell out Israel's covenant responsibilities.

The two tablets of stone containing the law were

carried in the ark, so when Israel followed the ark, they followed the visible reminder that God loved them and had committed Himself to them. When Jesus ate the last supper with His disciples, He lifted the cup and declared that His blood was the blood of the new covenant. By His death on the cross, Jesus has bound Himself to us and has made Himself available to our needs.

Any Christian can live in victory; but in order to do so, every Christian must obey.

A few years ago, several families from our church went to Colorado in early spring. Winter was hanging on, and the dozen trout lakes near our cabin were still frozen. One of my friends, who had lived in that area, suggested I walk out on one of the frozen lakes, commenting that it might be my only chance to walk on water. Where I came from, the ice never froze that solidly, and I wasn't too crazy about the idea. But they assured me all would be well; so I slowly ventured out, keeping close to the edge just in case I had to get back to safety in a hurry. It was a brief, nervous walk on the water.

Later as we drove past another of the lakes, I saw a fellow sitting on a wooden box right out in the middle. He was hunched over a hole in the ice, fishing! It was quite a lesson for me. That man had enough faith in the ice to sit in the middle unafraid and fish. Why? He lived nearby and *knew the ice*! He knew it, he trusted it; therefore, he submitted himself to it.

Any Christian can live in victory; but in order to do so, every Christian must obey. An old hymn says it like this:

> Trust and obey,
>   For there's no other way,
> To be happy in Jesus
>   But to trust and obey.[1]

Seven

IT'S THE FOLLOW-THROUGH
THAT COUNTS

I love to play tennis, but I have a big problem with my follow-through. When I hit the ball, instead of bringing the racket on through to complete the swing, I stop—and the ball sails out of bounds. I just can't remember to follow through. That's why I gave up golf. In every sport, following through seems to be necessary. A few days ago I was watching a Little League baseball game. The pitcher, who looked to be about seven or eight years old, was having a tough time getting the balls across. After a bad pitch his mother yelled from the bleachers, "Follow through, Greg! Follow through!" I keep hoping I'll find a sport that doesn't require follow-through.

I spent a lot of time looking for a spiritual experience like that too—you know, one that didn't require any follow-through. I prefer to be borne along effortlessly in my Christian walk. But that's not the way it works. And some great spiritual experiences faded into nothingness because I failed to follow through. For many, the Christian life is like a soap-box derby. Someone gives you a big shove down a steep hill, and you're sailing. The wind whistles in your ears, the people sweep by, and everything's great. Then suddenly you begin to slow down; you get slower and slower until finally you stop. You're stalled until you find another hill and someone to give you another push.

It's not how loud you shout or high you jump, but how you walk when you hit the ground.

A lot of folks are stalled in the wilderness, hoping God will come along and give them a big push that will propel them into a big, beautiful experience. The roadside is littered with countless Christians who used to be "really turned on" for the Lord. Most of them are there because they didn't follow through.

The Bible has a lot to say about this. Paul, for instance, emphasized the walk of the Christian: "As you therefore have received Christ Jesus the Lord, so walk in Him" (Col. 2:6). Most of us in our public testimonies stress our "crisis experience," but Paul talks about the walk. As the old preachers used to say, "It's not how loud you shout or high you jump, but how you walk when you hit the ground." Amen, brother.

The importance of follow-through is also seen in the

fact that only four chapters in Joshua deal with the actual entering of the land. The other twenty relate what happened after the entrance. And a very strange thing happened first. Because they were crossing at one of the most strongly fortified areas of Canaan, about forty thousand of the Israelites entered the land dressed for battle—but fighting was not their first act. Though they were vulnerable at that location and ready to fight, God ordered them to stop in that exposed area and worship Him by erecting a memorial. Each tribe was directed to take a stone from the middle of the river, one for each of the twelve tribes, and set them up in their encampment. This place became known as Gilgal—The Place of Passage. The stones, probably placed carefully in a circle, stood as a memorial to what God had done for His people that day.

The Israelites had had a great crisis experience and the strange circle of stones was their follow-through—and the guarantee that the experience would last. Investigating the meaning of these stones will provide some profitable help for our own program of follow-through. "What mean these stones?" (Josh. 4:21, KJV).

The Stones Were the Evidence of a Lasting Experience

The monument of stones was there "so that you may fear the LORD your God forever" (Josh. 4:24). The miracle of Jordan was to have a permanent effect on Israel. There was no doubt that the mighty display of divine power produced instant reverence for the Lord, but that experience was to be so deep, so intense, that such reverence would last forever. And, I must add, that reverence was to be independent of His miracles. In other words, if God had to keep performing miracles to sustain their reverence, the experience was defective.

It is impossible to have a genuine encounter with God and remain the same. Look at Moses. Meeting God at the burning bush revolutionized and reversed his whole life. Jacob's experience at Bethel wrought such a change in him God gave him a new name. The Damascus road confrontation turned Saul of Tarsus into Paul the apostle—a change so extraordinary that the Christians could not believe it at first. Those twelve stones proclaimed the beginning of a new era for Israel. But it was only a beginning. That first step must lengthen into a walk.

This aspect of Christian experience is a major thrust of the New Testament. Paul warned the Corinthians that any religious experience which didn't result in holy living was receiving the grace of God in vain (2 Cor. 6:1–4). The Galatians made a good start but were in danger of returning to their former religious rut. Staying free was as much a part of their salvation as being set free (Gal. 3:1–3; 5:1).

One of the most sobering statements of the Bible occurs in Philippians 2:16. Having admonished the Philippians to go on to maturity, Paul says, ". . . so that in the day of Christ I may have cause to glory because I did not run in vain nor toil in vain." What an astonishing thing to say. The fact they had been converted wasn't sufficient to cause Paul to glory when he stood before Christ. As far as he was concerned (and remember, he was writing under the inspiration of the Spirit), if they failed to follow through to maturity, his labor would be in vain. All his efforts would be meaningless. How could this be? Even if they didn't grow and develop, at least they would go to heaven. Surely that means something. Not much, Paul says. He felt that if his ministry to them achieved only their entrance into heaven, he might as well have stayed home. Of what use is a talent in the ground, a fig tree without fruit, a light under a basket? We desperately need to rid ourselves of the false idea that Christ shed His blood simply to buy our way into heaven.

The gospel is frequently described as dynamite, because we get the word from the Greek word *dunamis*, translated "power" in Romans 1:16. Unfortunately, some of our experiences are exactly like a stick of dynamite: a loud noise, a lot of dust stirred up, over in a second and not a trace left! We get another word from *dunamis* which I think better describes salvation. It is "dynamo," a continual source of energy. When God saved us, He placed within us a dynamo, the Holy Spirit, who provides an unceasing flow of divine energy, a permanent power supply that enables us to become all God saved us to be.

The Stones Were to Become the Center of Their Lives

From the very spot in the river where the priests had stood with the ark, from the heart of their experience, they took twelve stones and placed them in their camp. What God had done for them was to be an integral part of their daily lives. Gilgal, the site of the memorial, became the base of all their activities. From there they went out to fight, and whether victorious or defeated, they always returned to that sacred spot. It was the center of their life.

In the following through we need a Gilgal, *a place of remembering.* The stones, like our experience, reminded the people of the faithfulness of their covenant God. It's frightening to realize how easily we forget spiritual matters. We can remember a sordid joke we heard years ago but can't recall last Sunday's sermon text.

That's why the Bible frequently warns us about the dangers of forgetfulness. Thumb through the pages of Deuteronomy, for instance, and see how many such warnings are there. Here are some from the eighth chapter: "And you shall remember all the way which the Lord your God has led you. . . . Beware lest you forget the Lord your God by not keeping His commandments . . . lest, when you have eaten and are satisfied . . . you forget the Lord your God. . . . But you shall remember the Lord your God. . . . And it shall come about if you ever forget the Lord your God . . . you shall surely perish" (Deut. 8:2, 11–12, 14, 18–19).

There wasn't any danger they would forget crossing the Jordan and entering Canaan; the danger was that they would forget it had been accomplished by God's power alone. When that happened, they would take God for granted. Witness the defeat at Ai! We all have a tendency to forget our helplessness and God's omnipotence. That leads to living in the energy of our flesh, which in turn leads to disaster.

Jesus established the Lord's Supper as a remembrance of His death for us. That's why we call it the Memorial Supper—like the stones, it is a place of remembering. When we eat the bread and drink the cup, we do it remembering that it was for our sins His body was broken and His blood shed. Remembering the cross is a powerful deterrent to backsliding. Peter tells us that our lack of certain spiritual virtues is evidence we have forgotten our "purification from . . . former sins" (2 Pet. 1:9).

We also need *a place of readjustment.* Every Christian, sooner or later, experiences spiritual vertigo and becomes disoriented. Like Joshua, we need a place where we can realign ourselves with the purpose and will of God. D.L. Moody, the famous evangelist of the last century, retreated every summer to a private place where he could be alone with God and "retune the instrument." Even in the midst of religious activity, our hearts can grow cold, and though we may excuse ourselves because we're "working for the Lord," the heat of activity will not take the place of the warmth of communion.

How can we know we need readjusting? The standard by which we measure our present relationship with God is His previous work in us. We examine our present spiritual status in the light of that past experience. Why not check yourself right now? You remember how it was—the fresh awareness of His presence, the ever-present joy, the love that seemed to flow from your fingertips, the irresistible desire to talk about Him. Is it still that way? Is it more so? Or is it less? You used to be patient; now you're touchy and irritable. Moodiness has replaced joyfulness. Worry and anxiety have replaced peace and contentment. Do you find yourself trying to live up to what you were? If so, you need to return to Gilgal, the place of readjustment, the place of confession and forgiveness.

Do you find yourself trying to live up to what you were? If so, you need to return to Gilgal, the place of confession and forgiveness.

William Cowper may have been speaking for you when he wrote:

> Where is the blessedness I knew
> When first I saw the Lord?
> Where is the soul-refreshing view
> Of Jesus and His Word?
>
> What peaceful hours I then enjoyed!
> How sweet their mem'ry still!
> But they have left an aching void
> The world can never fill.

Return, O Holy Dove, return
>   Sweet messenger of rest;
I hate the sins that made Thee mourn
>   And drove Thee from my breast.[2]

One of my closest friends is a pilot. Sometime ago he flew me to a Bible conference in a private plane. I'm a sort of frustrated pilot, and after we took off and were settled on course, I asked if I could take the controls. I thought I was doing pretty well until he tapped me on the shoulder and pointed at the compass. Without realizing it, I had drifted far off course. In the same way, if we're not careful, we will assume we're right on the beam spiritually when in fact we are drifting off course.

The Stones Were a Witness to Others

It has been said that you can't meet God and not know it. That's true. And others will know it too. When Moses came away from the presence of God, his face glowed with the glory of that encounter—and the people saw it. Describing the mercy of God, the psalmist wrote, "And He put a new song in my mouth, a song of praise to our God; many will see and fear, and will trust in the LORD" (Ps. 40:3). There's an unusual song—you *see* it instead of hearing it. Neither the psalmist nor Moses had to convince people they had met God. Moses didn't need a glow-in-the-dark bumper sticker that said, "I'm Living in the Sonshine." Badges, beads and bumper stickers are fine, but if it takes those things to show I'm a Christian, then I'm not much of one.

We have an obligation to those around us and to those who come after us. Three times in Joshua chapter 4, the people were commanded to explain the meaning of the stones when their children asked about them.

Our transformed lives should be causing people to ask, "What does this mean?"

That tells me that there ought to be something in our lives that makes people ask questions. Usually, in our witnessing efforts the most difficult problem is how to get started, how to bring the subject up without offending. Some Christians wear curious looking pins hoping someone will ask them what it means and their prepared answer will open the door to witness. There's nothing wrong with that, but it ought to be our Christlike life and not a pin that causes folks to ask questions. The apostle Peter told his readers, "Sanctify Christ as Lord in your hearts, always being ready to make a defense to everyone who asks you to give an account for the hope that is in you" (1 Pet. 3:15). If Jesus is Lord, be ready, for sooner or later someone is going to ask you about it.

While Peter was delivering his well-prepared sermon, the congregation interrupted him, crying, "What must we do?" What preacher wouldn't like to have that kind of response! Do you know what made them do that? It wasn't only Peter's sermon. They had seen something earlier in the behavior of the Christians that caused them to ask, "What does this mean?" It was the transformed lives of the believers that attracted their attention so Peter could preach to them.

It was the same with the Philippian jailer. He had been so impressed with the way Paul and Silas reacted to their mistreatment and imprisonment that when God shook the foundations for them, he brought up the subject.

But here is the significant thing about the stones. They were the past reaching into the present, a present condition resulting from a past event. It's all right to talk about the past if there is some evidence of that past in the present. Every once in a while someone says to me, "You should have seen this church fifteen years ago. God sent a great revival—it was really something!" When I hear that, I feel like saying, "Well, I'm glad you told me; otherwise, I'd never have known it." There's nothing wrong with talking about the past—it's good to remember and recite God's past blessings. But here's the point: there ought to be *present* evidence of those past blessings. That past work of God should have been the beginning of an experience that is still going on.

Before we leave this subject, notice that each tribe had a stone. This says to me that every family ought to have a memorial of God's blessings. As the head of each tribe was responsible for getting the stone, the head of each family should be able to bring a stone representing his experience with the Lord as a witness to his family.

There ought to be in his life something that makes his children ask about his experience with the Lord.

When the stones were properly placed, God said they would be a witness to all the world: "that all the peoples of the earth may know that the hand of the LORD is mighty" (Josh. 4:24).

And as we learn to follow through with our experience and go on to maturity in Christ, we will become a memorial to the mighty, saving hand of our Lord.

Eight

WHY WE FAIL TO GROW

Billy Sunday used to say, "If we Christians were as weak physically as we are spiritually, we would all need crutches." The colorful baseball player-turned-evangelist was saying that if you're not growing spiritually, you ought to be worried. Growth is the normal and natural result of life; and if there isn't growth, that life is in jeopardy. We're not surprised when we grow physically; we expect it. If, by chance, growth doesn't occur, we immediately know something is wrong and attempt to uncover the problem.

And yet we often look upon Christians who have grown and are growing as extraordinary specimens of Christianity. As a pastor, I was always excitedly surprised to find members who were really spiritual. They became the major sites of interest I pointed out to visiting ministers, who never failed to share my excitement and coveted the same phenomenon for their own church. But if

I had driven him around town pointing out this fellow who had grown an inch in the last year and that one who had gained five pounds, he would have thought me crazy.

I believe as Christians we have no right to call ourselves normal until spiritual growth becomes as natural as physical growth. The apostle John prayed that his friend Gaius would prosper and be in good health, "just as your soul prospers" (3 John 2). Would you want someone to pray the same thing for you? Frankly, if our physical and financial prosperity were determined by our spiritual prosperity, we would probably be crippled bankrupts.

We do not simply drift into maturity. To grow we must swim upstream against the stubborn currents that try to hold us back.

If growth is the normal consequence of life, then where's the problem? Just as there are enemies to physical growth, there are also enemies to spiritual growth. Our spiritual development is never unopposed. We do not simply drift into maturity. To grow we must swim upstream against the stubborn currents that try to hold us back. In the last chapter we discussed the follow-through of the Christian life. We saw that every authentic experience is a lasting one with continuing results.

Okay, you accept that and desire it, but it isn't happening. You know your experience was real, and there has been some progress, but it is pitifully small, almost microscopic. What's the problem?

The answer is the subject of this chapter. In this respect, the seventeenth chapter of Joshua contains an instructive story. The people have entered the land and now, according to God's instructions, Joshua is dividing it among the people. In the fourteenth verse we hear a complaint from some of the tribes: "Then the sons of Joseph spoke to Joshua, saying, 'Why have you given me only one lot and one portion for an inheritance, since I am a numerous people whom the LORD has thus far blessed?'"

Note the significant phrase "thus far." They are saying that in the past God had been good to them; up to this point the Lord has blessed them. The phrase implies some doubt about God's blessing from here on. Sounds like some of us, doesn't it? "The Lord used to bless me, but something's happened; for a while everything was going just great, but now . . ."

Get out your Bible and read Joshua 17:12–18. This passage throws some light on why we fail to grow.

We Fail to Grow When We Exercise Partial Conquest

There's a telling statement in verses 12 and 13: "But the sons of Manasseh could not take possession of these cities, because the Canaanites persisted in living in that land. And it came about when the sons of Israel became strong, they put the Canaanites to forced labor, *but they did not drive them out completely.*"

Now don't miss this point: although Israel had conquered the land, many of the Canaanites—the enemy, if you please—still lived there. In Joshua 16:10 we read, "But they [Manasseh and Ephraim] did not drive out the Canaanites who lived in Gezer, so the Canaanites live in the midst of Ephraim to this day, and they became forced laborers." And over in Judges chapter 1 we discover an important clue concerning their problem:

> But Manasseh did not take possession of Beth-shean . . . so the Canaanites persisted in living in that land. And it came about when Israel became strong, that they put the Canaanites to forced labor, but they did not drive them out completely. Neither did Ephraim drive out the Canaanites. . . . Zebulun did not drive out the inhabitants. . . . Asher did not drive out the inhabitants. . . . Naphtali did not drive out the inhabitants. . . . (Judg. 1:27–31, 33)

Before Israel entered the land, God specified in no uncertain terms that all the inhabitants of the land were to be driven out completely—not a single Canaanite was to be left. But again and again with monotonous significance, we read that they did not drive them out. Now the land teemed with both natives and newcomers. No wonder they complained of crowded conditions!

Suppose you meet me on the street and ask me how I am.

"Not so well," I answer. "We need a larger house. There are only four of us, but we're crowded."

"I can help you," you say. "There's a twelve-room

house for sale real cheap. A family of seven has lived there but they're wanting to move."

"Thanks, I'll look into it." Off I go and buy the house and move my wife and two children into the twelve rooms.

A few days later you meet me again on the street and ask how I am.

"No so well," I answer. "We need a larger house."

"A larger house? But there are only four of you in that twelve-room castle! How could you be crowded?"

"Well, the former owners—seven of them, you know—are still living there, and it's pretty crowded."

It wouldn't require a genius to solve my problem. Move out the former owners! What right do I have to complain about crowded conditions when I am not using the room I have?

And that was exactly the case with the complaining tribes. They had plenty of room—but it was occupied

Have you allowed some Canaanites (sinful habits) to remain in your life? There can be no continuing growth as long as you tolereate the presence of a single one.

by the enemy. You see, it's foolish to ask God to give you more blessings when you haven't lived out the blessings you already have.

No use asking God for additional truth when you haven't obeyed what you already know. My friend Manley Beasley was speaking to a ministers' meeting when he suddenly stopped and closed his Bible with this exclamation: "That's enough preaching. You know more now than you're living up to!"

Painfully true.

Let me put it to you in the phrase Allen Redpath used to describe this incident. "Are you living up to your capacity?" Look around; have you allowed some Canaanites to remain in your life? God told you to drive out every one, but there were two or three you were especially fond of, and so you've allowed them to hang around. Of course, you've given them strict orders to behave themselves—and for the most part they've done so. Let me tell you, there can be no continuing growth as long as you tolerate the presence of a single Canaanite.

It's interesting to note some of the reasons we keep Canaanites around:

A Spirit of Compromise. God said that every inhabitant had to go. We reason that surely one or two won't make any difference. That's the way it begins. We know a thing is wrong—but just a little bit. And after all, no one is perfect; we know of worse things in some other Christians, and they seem to get along okay. But no matter how we say it, we are compromising the Word of God, and that is plain, unadulterated disobedience.

A Spirit of Complacency. Did you notice that when the tribes allowed the Canaanites to stay, they put them to forced labor? That means they made slaves of them. Sure, they were the enemy, but now they were slaves and under control.

Who says the Bible isn't up-to-date? I can't count

the number of people I've heard reason the same way. "Yeah, I know it's not altogether right—but I can handle it. It's a problem, but I've learned to control it." Have you ever heard someone say about his drinking, "Oh, I can take it or leave it"? What's so great about that? That's all anyone can do—take it or leave it. There is no third alternative. But I have observed that those who say that usually choose to "take it."

The truth is, you can't handle it. Canaanites refuse to be slaves.

A Spirit of Cowardice. If it weren't so tragic, this would be funny. Joshua had told the people that if they wanted more room, they should go up to the forest and clear the land. Here's their reply: "And the sons of Joseph said, 'The hill country is not enough for us, and all the Canaanites who live in the valley have chariots of iron'" (17:16).

There's the real reason. First they said that the hill country wasn't big enough, but actually they were afraid of the armed Canaanites. But I thought the Canaanites had been put to forced labor? I thought they were slaves and under control? If so, then those are the strangest slaves I've ever heard of.

Years ago I heard this story. I don't know whether it's true but it's good. It seems that during a heavy battle, a captain commanded his lieutenant to pull back to a certain position.

The lieutenant replied, "I can't, sir."

"Why not?" the captain asked.

"I've taken a prisoner, sir."

"Bring him with you."

"He won't come, sir."

"Well, leave him and come yourself!"

"He won't let me, sir."

One of the big reasons we don't try to drive out the Canaanites (these pet sins and hidden habits) is that we're afraid we can't. We avoid a direct confrontation. It's much more comfortable living with the illusion that we can drive them out any time we please. You say you can quit that habit any time you want to—why don't you, then? Is it possible that you're the real slave?

A Spirit of Covetousness. "They put the Canaanites to forced labor." Why drive them all out? They make good workers—and cheap labor. It could be very advantageous to keep a few of them around.

How does this apply to us? Here's a businessman who realizes that it is the Lord who gives him the power to gain wealth, that it is actually His business, so he decides to operate on Christian principles. But in case God doesn't come through, he keeps a Canaanite of worldly business tactics in the back room. Or perhaps a teenager commits himself to Christ and wants Him to occupy first place in every area of his life. But it may be that being a Christian won't bring him everything he wants in popularity and pleasure, and so on occasions he resorts to a Canaanite of doubtful behavior. Maybe a pastor has decided that the gimmicks and gadgets he has been using to attract people to his church aren't Christ-honoring. From now on his ministry will be conducted solely on the principles the Holy Spirit approves. But the immediate visible results he hoped for don't come. He was afraid that might happen and cleverly kept one or two of the old Canaanite gimmicks around. They will build up that attendance in no time at all.

> *At this pecise moment we are as spiritual as we really want to be.*

I think that's enough said. Are you living up to your capacity?

We Fail to Grow When We Expect Preferential Consideration

Manasseh was the first-born of Joseph; the Ephraimites were relatives of Joshua, the head man. Surely they deserved special treatment. You couldn't expect someone as great as they were to live by the same rules as everyone else. It was the VIP treatment for them.

I'm amazed at how many believers actually feel this way. They know the laws governing growth and spirituality—faithful Bible study and prayer, up-to-date confession of sin, diligent obedience to the Word of God, God's glory desired in all things. And yet they expect God's blessings without them. As far as they're concerned, they have been lifted above the disciplines of discipleship. I've counseled with Christians who had lost the joy of their salvation and wanted to recover it but refused to submit themselves to those disciplines. They were searching for an "experience" that would catapult them effortlessly back into a right relationship with God.

Our passage reveals two factors that contribute to this attitude:

Arrogance. The sons of Joseph boasted that they were a great people and had been singularly blessed by the Lord. This, they thought, should qualify them for preferential treatment.

Pride is an insidious termite that eats away the foundation of Christian growth. It can attack a denomination, a church or an individual with equal deadliness. A denomination may assume it's great because it's big; a church because it's wealthy; a person because he's talented. Blessings can easily become curses. A respected position in the church, widely acclaimed talent, past blessings, high honors—any one of these can inflate us with the hot air of arrogance.

Indolence. This was touched upon in chapter 2 but bears repeating. I'm convinced the main reason Christians are not more spiritual, more mature, more dedicated is that they are too lazy! That's right—the major problem with most Christians is laziness. It was so with the crowd in Joshua 17. Joshua told them if they wanted more land, they could have it if they were willing to work for it. Cut down the trees and drive out the Canaanites were the only stipulations. But that's exactly what they weren't willing to do. They didn't want to build or battle; they just wanted to beg. And we're often the same way. At this precise moment we are as spiritual as we really want to be. Oh, I know, we moan and groan, wishing we were more spiritual, but wishing won't get it. It's useless to beg God for more growth if we're not willing to build and battle for it.

One day a father took his son to Spurgeon's College to study for the ministry under that prince of preachers. When Mr. Spurgeon told the father the course of instruction would require several years, the father said, "My son is an unusually bright young man. I'm certain you could arrange for him to finish much sooner."

Mr. Spurgeon replied, "Sir, God takes twenty years to grow an oak tree and only six months to grow a squash. Which do you want your son to be?"

There are no shortcuts to maturity. To reach it demands discipline and determination. And that's what we are going to discuss now.

We Fail to Grow When We Evade Priority Commitments

Here was Joshua's solution to their problem:

And Joshua spoke to the house of Joseph, to Ephraim and Manasseh, saying, "You are a numerous people and have great power; you shall not have one lot only, but the hill country shall be yours. For though it is a forest, you shall clear it, and to its farthest borders it shall be yours; for you shall drive out the Canaanites, even though they have chariots of iron and though they are strong." (Josh. 17:17–18)

Clear out the forest and drive out the Canaanites. That was the simple solution to their growth problem. But as we've already seen in the first chapter of Judges, they refused to accept this answer. Priority number one, according to Joshua, was to accomplish these two things. Until then no expansion could be expected. The land was theirs but before they could possess it, these things had to be done. So it is with us.

You will never find time for God; you will have to make time.

Although they evaded this priority commitment, I trust we will not; so let's examine more closely the two tasks Joshua assigned to them. I call them priority commitments for growth, as necessary to our growth as they were to theirs.

1. *We must clear out the harmless things that clutter our lives.* The first step was the clearing of the forest. Now there's nothing wrong with trees; they are a beautiful and useful part of God's creation. But if they occupy the ground you want to build your home upon, they have to go. Building your home is a priority commitment, and in order to fulfill it, you must clear the land.

The trees symbolize the many harmless things, even good things, that fill the agenda of our daily lives. I'm certain that when we've talked about the necessity of a daily time of prayer and Bible study, someone has said, "Oh, that would be great, but I'm just too busy. I don't have room for another thing in my day." The truth is, we all have the same amount of time, twenty-four hours to the day and seven days to the week. I find that people usually manage to make time for what they think is really important. And if you don't have time to do everything God intends you to do, it simply means that you are misusing some of your time.

There is time to do everything you are supposed to do. The trouble is that most of us are so *busy being good, we don't have time to be godly.*

In Matthew 13 Jesus described this situation in the parable of the sower. It is really a parable of the soil, for the soil is the main subject of the story. The part that concerns us tells about the seed that fell into thorny ground: "And others fell among the thorns, and the thorns came up and choked them out" (13:7). Jesus explains the meaning in verse 22: "And the one on whom seed was sown among the thorns, this is the man who hears the word, and the worry of the world, and the deceitfullness of riches choke the word, and it becomes unfruitful." The ground of his life was so cluttered with the cares of this world, the Word of God was strangled before it had a chance to grow. What a description of so many! No wonder the Word of God never produces anything fruitful and lasting in their lives—it can't compete with the thorns.

You will never *find* time for God; you will have to *make* time. This means some trees will have to be cut down. Perhaps late-night television will have to be eliminated so you can rise earlier in order to have time to pray and read the Word. That's only an example of what I mean. If you really want to know, God will show you the trees you need to clear away.

2. *We must clean out the harmful things that corrupt our lives.* After the trees come the Canaanites. Let me point out something interesting. It would seem more reasonable to drive out the Canaanites first. After all, do you think they're going to lounge around watching us chop down those trees? Why, all the Canaanites in the world will come swooping down upon us. It will be another Little Big Horn! But no, Joshua had the order correct. Cut down the trees; then you will be able to drive out the enemy.

You will never have the power to drive out the habits and hang-over sins in your life until you give priority to a daily time of fellowship and communion with God. Once you have accomplished this, the divine strength you receive will enable you to drive out the enemy. Remember, in Joshua 7 we saw that although Israel entered the land ready to fight, the first thing God had them do was worship. That's the divine order: *worship before warfare.*

The principle of growth lives within every believer, but as with our physical development, we must cooperate with the laws of spiritual health if that growth is to be realized.

Epilogue

WILL IT LAST?

When I began to experience this victorious life, my first question was, "Will it last?" I had had plenty of mountaintop experiences that made me think, "This is it! At last I've found what I've been looking for." But none of them lasted. After a couple of weeks, they would fizzle out like a firecracker that won't explode, and I would find myself once again in the valley of despair. And each episode left my valley a little deeper and a little darker.

But I have made the joyful discovery that the real thing does last. And it doesn't merely last, but grows bigger and better. I no longer have to lug buckets of water from the wells of other men—Jesus has given me an artesian well that requires neither bucket nor rope. The living waters spring up to meet me. It is a well that never runs dry, even in the darkest moments of life. In the years since that experience of entering in, I have trudged through a desert where no water was, where no flowers grew, where cherished voices no longer greeted me—but the well was there. I am happy to report that through disappointment, frustration, heartbreak, tragedy and death, the experience has lasted. And today my knowledge of, fellowship with and joy in Jesus is sweeter than ever before. I expect it to be even more so tomorrow.

I heard about two little boys on an ocean voyage. They were standing at the rail of the ship staring at the vast expanse of endless water. One said, "Wow, look at all that water." The other replied, "Yeah, and that's only the top!" And in the Christian life, this life of victory, we have only touched the top. There is more to Jesus than any of us has ever experienced, and throughout eternity we will drink deeper and deeper from the inexhaustible fountain of His matchless grace.

The book is ended, but the journey is not. It will end like this:

> Who is this who comes to meet me
>   On the desert way,
> As the Morning Star foretelling
>   God's unclouded day?
> He it is who came to win me
>   On the cross of shame;
> In His glory well I know Him
>   Evermore the same.

Oh the blessed joy of meeting,
    All the desert past!
Oh the wondrous word of greeting
    He shall speak at last!
He and I together entering
    Those fair courts above—
He and I together sharing
    All the Father's love.

Where no shade nor stain can enter,
    Nor the gold be dim,
In that holiness unsullied,
    I shall walk with Him.
Meet companion then for Jesus,
    From Him, for Him made—
Glory of God's grace forever
    There in me displayed.

He who in His hour of sorrow
    Bore the curse alone;
I who through lonely desert
    Trod where He had gone;
He and I, in that bright glory,
    One deep joy shall share—
Mine, to be forever with Him;
    His, that I am there.[3]

Endnotes

1. John H. Sammis, "Trust and Obey" (hymn), 1887, public domain.

2. William Cowper, "O For a Closer Walk with God," in Richard Conyers, *Collection of Psalms and Hymns* (London, 1772), public domain.

3. Frances Ridley Havergal, "The Welcome to the King," in *Coming to the King* (Boston: E.P. Dutton, 1880), public domain.

This book was produced by CLC Publications. We hope it has been life-changing and has given you a fresh experience of God through the work of the Holy Spirit. CLC Publications is an reach of CLC Ministries International, a global literature mission with work in over fifty countries. If you would like to know more about us or are interested in opportunities to serve with a faith mission, we invite you to contact us at:

CLC Ministries International
PO Box 1449
Fort Washington, PA 19034

Phone: 215-542-1242
E-mail: orders@clcpublications.com
Website: www.clcpublications.com

DO YOU LOVE GOOD CHRISTIAN BOOKS?
Do you have a heart for worldwide missions?

You can receive a FREE subscription to
CLC's newsletter on global literature missions
Order by e-mail at:

clcworld@clcusa.org
Or fill in the coupon below and mail to:

PO Box 1449
Fort Washington, PA 19034

FREE *CLC WORLD* SUBSCRIPTION!

Name: _____

Address:_____

_____

Phone: _____ E-mail:_____

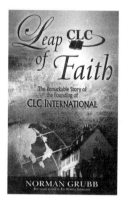